English Language Arts

Activity Book 1

2

Book Staff and Contributors

Kristen Kinney-Haines *Director, English Language Arts*
Amy Rauen *Director, Instructional Design*
Susan Raley *Text Editor*
Tricia Battipede *Senior Creative Manager*
Julie Jankowski *Senior Visual Designer*
Caitlin Gildrien *Visual Designer*
Sheila Smith *Visual & Cover Designer*
Dale-Marie Bryan, Alane Gernon-Paulsen, Amy Losi *Writers*
Amy Eward *Content Specialist; Senior Manager, Writing and Editing*
Dan Smith *Senior Project Manager*

Doug McCollum *Senior Vice President, Product Development*
Kristin Morrison *Vice President, Design and Product Management*
Kelly Engel *Senior Director, Curriculum*
Christopher Frescholtz *Senior Director, Program Management*
Erica Castle *Senior Director, Creative Design*
Lisa Dimaio Iekel *Senior Production Manager*

Image Credits

All illustrations © Stride, Inc., unless otherwise noted.

Characters
Tommy DiGiovanni, Matt Fedor, Ben Gamache, Shannon Palmer

Cover Illustration
Helen Musselwhite

Interior Pattern
Spiral. © Silmen/iStock.

Interior Images
Book 1 **23** Illustrations by Danielle Pioli from *Zara's Big Messy Day (That Turned Out Okay)* by Rebekah Borucki. **210** Honeybee and flowers. © nataka/iStock.

ISBN: 978-1-60153-608-2

Printed by Bradford & Bigelow, Newburyport, MA, USA, May 2021.

Table of Contents

Problems and Solutions

Bears

Interesting People

Think About Reading:
What Do You Do With a Problem? (A)

Fill in the book information.

Title: What DO You DO With A Problem?

Author: Kobi Yamada

Illustrator: Mae Besom

Answer the question.

Have you ever had a big problem? Write or draw a picture about that time.

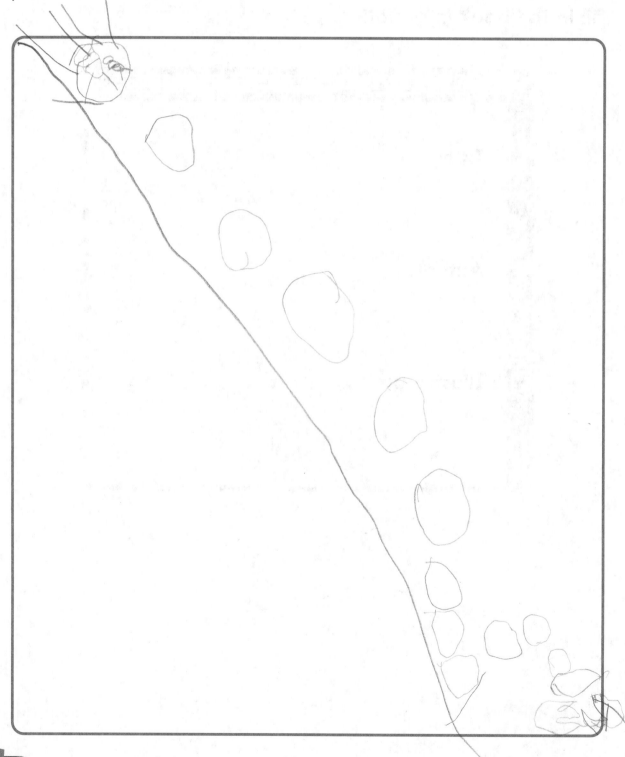

WHAT DO YOU DO WITH A PROBLEM? (A)

How Do You Feel?

Answer the questions.

1. How does the child feel at the beginning of the story? Write some words that describe how the child feels.

   Sad surprised worried Alot

2. Pretend you met the child at the beginning of the story. What would you say to the child? Write or draw your answer.

Begin and End a Sentence

A **sentence** is a complete thought.

- We begin a sentence with a **capital letter**.

- We end a sentence with an **end mark**. The end mark is often a **period**.

Circle what is incorrect about each sentence.

1. rain fell from the sky.

2. Lita and I put on our boots

3. my boots are red

Add a capital letter and period to each sentence.
The first one has been done for you.

4. <u>W</u>e jumped in the puddles <u>.</u>

5. ___ater splashed on us___

6. ___y boots got muddy and wet___

7. ___uddles are a lot of fun___

Complete each sentence.

8. _____ is my favorite part of school ___

9. I feel excited about _____ ___

Identify a Complete Sentence

A **complete sentence** has a naming part and an action part.

- We call the naming part the **subject**.

- We call the action part the **predicate**.

For each sentence, underline the subject one time. Underline the predicate two times. The first one has been done for you.

1. My friend Moira dribbled the basketball.

2. Shaunda painted a sunset.

3. The kitten purred.

4. I slept for hours.

Think about *What Do You Do With a Problem?*

5. Underline the subject once and the predicate twice.

   The child felt brave at the end of the story.

6. Complete the sentence.

I felt brave when _____

_____

Color each shape that has a complete sentence.

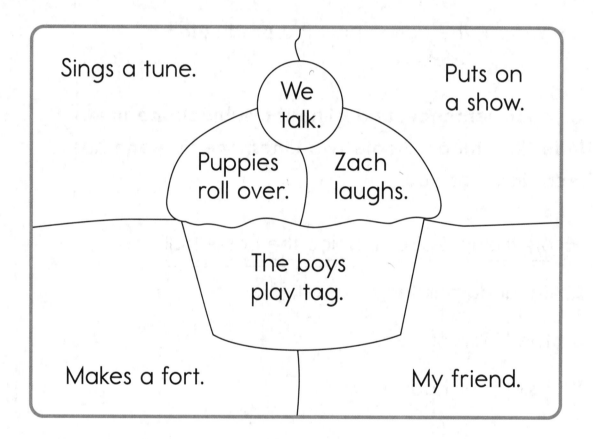

Answer the riddle.

7. What kind of cup can't hold water?

_____

Spelling List 1

Cut out the headings and spelling words. Lay out the headings. Then sort the words by their sound and spelling pattern. After sorting, keep your cutouts in a safe place.

/ă/ hat	grade
/ā/ cake	have
oddball	mad
back	made
brave	man
crash	mane
fast	want
gave	

Write a Statement

A **statement** is a telling sentence.

• We begin a statement with a **capital letter**.

• We end a statement with a **period**.

Read each statement aloud.

• **Underline the capital letter.**

• **Circle the period.**

1. The dog eats the bone.

2. Its spots are black.

Put a ✓ next to each statement.

3. My pet is in the woods. ✓

4. Is that your dog? ___

5. Tim and I run after Wags. ✓

Complete each statement.

6. My favorite animal is _____

7. _____ makes me feel happy.

Think about *What Do You Do With a Problem?*
The character pictures a problem as a dark cloud.

• Draw how *you* picture a problem.

• Write a *statement* about your drawing.

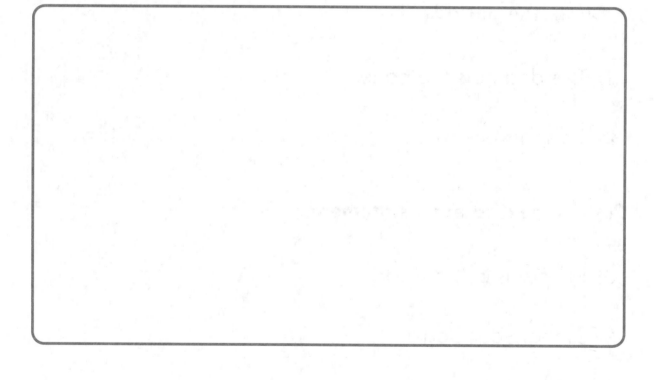

Practice: Spelling List 1

Get your spelling cutouts. Set up the headings, and sort the spelling words again.

Look at your sort, and write down each spelling word under the correct heading on the chart.

/ă/ hat	/ā/ cake	oddball

Do one of the following activities to practice your spelling words:

Write sentences.

Choose four of your spelling words. Write a sentence using each word.

Write part of a story.

Choose four of your spelling words. Write part of a story using the four words.

_____

_____

_____

_____

_____

_____

WHAT DO YOU DO WITH A PROBLEM? (C)

Think About Reading:
Zara's Big Messy Day (A)

Fill in the book information.

Title: Zara's Big Messy Day (That turned out okay)

Author:

Illustrator:

Make a prediction.

What do you think will happen in the story *Zara's Big Messy Day?*

_____

_____

_____

_____

_____

_____

ZARA'S BIG MESSY DAY (A)

Who Am I?

Follow the instructions to show your social identity.

1. How do you think of yourself? How do others see you? Fill in the chart on the next page. Write at least 5 parts of your identity. Add more circles if you need to. An example chart has been done for Zara.

Example:

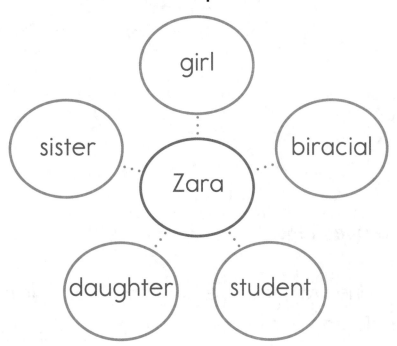

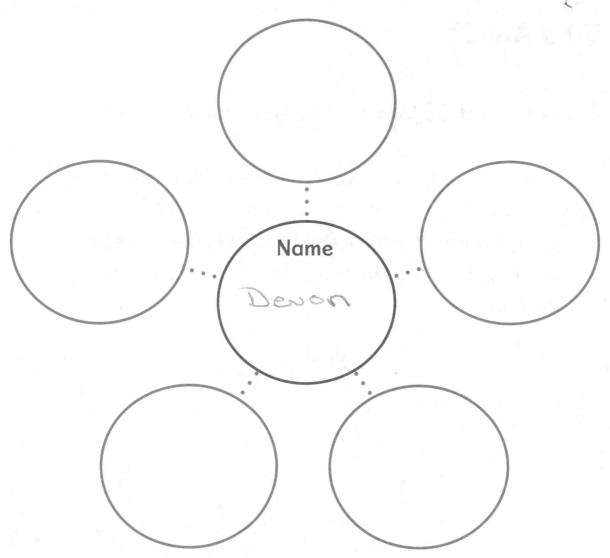

Name

Devon

Answer the questions.

2. What is one way you are like Zara? Put a ★ in
that circle on your chart.

3. What is one way you are different from Zara?
Put a ✔ in that circle on your chart.

Write a Question

A **question** is an asking sentence.

- We begin a question with a **capital letter**.

- We end a question with a **question mark**.

Read each question aloud.

- **Underline the capital letter.**

- **Circle the question mark.**

1. Why do dogs wag their tails?

2. Is a wolf a dog?

Put a ✓ next to the question. Put an X next to the statement.

3. How many toes do puppies have? ___

4. Puppies are cute animals. ___

Complete each question.

Common Question Words

who	what	where	when	why	how
will	can	do	is	are	did

5. _____ is your favorite sport ___

6. _____ do squirrels make their nests ___

7. _____ you do any silly tricks ___

Think about *Zara's Big Messy Day*.

8. Write a **question** to a character from the book.

Character: _____

Question: _____

_____

Apply: Spelling List 1

Answer the question. Then complete the chart.

1. What have you learned about words with the sound /ă/ like in *hat* and the sound /ā/ like in *cake*?

_____

_____

_____

_____

Do you think my hat looks like a cake?

2. Write each word where it goes in the chart.

| face | hand | make | ran | slam | what |

/ă/ hat	/ā/ cake	oddball

ZARA'S BIG MESSY DAY (A)

What Happens When?

Cut out each story box. Put the parts of the story in order on the next page.

Zara helps herself feel better when she wants to throw blocks at Sam. She smells the flowers and blows out the candles.

Now Zara knows that she can help herself feel better when she gets upset.

Zara gets angry when Sam spills juice all over her.

Glue the story boxes in the correct order.

Beginning

Middle

End

Write an Exclamation

An **exclamation** shows strong feelings.

- We begin an exclamation with a **capital letter**.
- We end an exclamation with an **exclamation mark**.

Read each exclamation aloud.

- Underline the capital letter.

- Circle the exclamation mark.

1. That is an awesome story!

2. Leo can do a one-handed cartwheel!

3. Millipedes have so many legs!

4. I finished the whole book!

Put a ✓ next to each exclamation.

5. Do goldfish have gills? ___

6. We are going to be late! ___

7. This is the best day of my life! ___

8. A week has seven days. ___

Complete each exclamation.

9. _____ is an amazing book ___

10. _____ should read it right now ___

Think about *Zara's Big Messy Day*. Penelope laughed at Zara's shoes.

11. Write an **exclamation** that you could say to Penelope. Then read your exclamation aloud.

_____

_____

Write a Command

A **command** is an order or a request.

- We begin a command with a **capital letter**.

- We end most commands with a **period**.

- We end a strong command with an **exclamation mark**.

Read each command aloud.

- Underline the capital letter.

- Circle the period or exclamation mark.

1. Look at the block tower.

2. Stop it right now!

3. Please help with the dishes.

4. Take a deep breath.

Put a ✓ next to each command.

5. My cousin is six years old. ___

6. Brush your teeth twice a day. ___

7. I love that movie! ___

8. Please help your brother. ___

Think about *Zara's Big Messy Day*.

9. Mama tells Zara, "Close your eyes. Smell the flowers. Blow out the candles."

Imagine you have a friend who is feeling angry. Write a **command** that you could say to that friend. Then read your command aloud.

_____

_____

10. Think about **retelling** the story. Put a ✔ next to **two** sentences that go in a retelling.

   a. Zara gets upset at breakfast. ___

   b. Get away from my tower, Sam! ___

   c. Who was mean to Zara? ___

   d. Zara and Mama talk about her day. ___

   e. Chinese food is my favorite! ___

11. Retell the story aloud to someone near you. Use the sentences you marked with a ✔ in your retelling.

12. What types of sentences did you use to retell the story? Circle the types. Explain your answer aloud to someone near you.

   statements   questions   exclamations   commands

Spelling List 2

Cut out the headings and spelling words. Lay out the headings. Then sort the words by their sound and spelling pattern. After sorting, keep your cutouts in a safe place.

/ĭ/ *pig*	grin
/ī/ *kite*	pride
oddball	smile
climb	still
five	twist
gift	wish
give	write

Write Four Sentences

Read each prompt.

- State what type of sentence you will use to answer. Use each sentence type one time.

- Write your sentence.

Types of Sentences

statement   question   exclamation   command

1. Shout something that makes you happy.

   a. My answer will be a(n) _____ .

   b. My answer: _____

   _____

2. Ask your teacher something.

   a. My answer will be a(n) _____ .

   b. My answer: _____

   _____

3. Tell what you love to learn about.

    a. My answer will be a(n) _____.

    b. My answer: _____

    _____

4. Give a friend advice on how to have a great day.

    a. My answer will be a(n) _____.

    b. My answer: _____

    _____

Practice: Spelling List 2

Get your spelling cutouts. Set up the headings, and sort the spelling words again.

Look at your sort, and write down each spelling word under the correct heading on the chart.

/ĭ/ pig	/ī/ kite	oddball

Do one of the following activities to practice your spelling words:

Draw and label.

Choose four of your spelling words. Draw a picture for each word. Then write the word under the picture.

Create a comic strip.

Create four panels of a comic strip. Draw pictures and write text with four or more of your spelling words.

All About Alliteration

Read the tongue twister. Then answer the question about it.

> Little lambs love to eat leaves.

1. Which letter is being used to create alliteration? Circle the answer.

s   l   t

Use alliteration to write your own tongue twister. The first words have been provided.

2. Many monkeys _____

_____

Draw a picture of what the monkeys are doing.

Circle the rhyming words in the poem. Then fill in the blanks to write your own poem.

The Sea

by Anonymous

I love the sea,
So peaceful and free.
Let's go for a swim
With my friend Kim.

Title _____

by _____

I love _____ ,

So peaceful and _____

Let's go for _____

With my friend _____ .

Apply: Spelling List 2

Answer the question.

1. What have you learned about words with the vowel *i* like *pig* and *kite*?

   _____

   _____

   _____

Do the word hunt.

2. Circle words with short i and long i spelling patterns.

   Min went for a swim. There was wind, but the ocean felt fine. Then, Min saw the fin of a big fish. She got a bit scared, so she swam in a line to the shore. She felt like it took a long time to get there. But, it only took nine minutes. When she looked for the big fish, she saw that her eyes had played a trick on her. It was only a rock.

Theme Time: Problems and Solutions

Think about the child in *What Do You Do With a Problem?* and Zara in *Zara's Big Messy Day.* Then answer the questions.

1. Both the child and Zara had a problem. How did the child and Zara feel about their problems?

The child felt _____

_____

Zara felt _____

_____

2. What is one thing you learned from the child or Zara that can help you when you have a problem?

I learned _____

_____

_____

(Optional) Complete the mini-project.

Zara learned a way to breathe that made herself feel better when she felt angry or upset. She did these steps:

Close your eyes.

Smell the flowers.

Blow out the candles.

You can use those steps, too. Make a poster to help yourself remember the steps.

Instructions:

1. Get a sheet of paper and markers or crayons.

2. On the paper, write the steps that Zara learned.

3. Make pictures that show what to do for each step.

4. Hang your poster up somewhere you can see it.

PROBLEMS AND SOLUTIONS WRAP-UP (A)

Go Write! and Set a Goal

Respond to the prompt. Or, write about a topic of your choice!

Prompt: What was your favorite story or poem from the unit? Why?

My Journal

PROBLEMS AND SOLUTIONS WRAP-UP (B)

A goal is something that you want to do.

You are getting ready to start a new unit. Choose one goal for yourself as a reader or writer. Or, write your own goal.

My GOAL!

- ☐ Read each book twice.
- ☐ Read for 10 minutes a day.
- ☐ Read to someone in my family.
- ☐ Use complete sentences in my writing.
- ☐ _____

_____

Write one thing you can do to help reach your goal.

I will _____

_____

Think About Reading:
Arnold and Louise: Lost and Found (A)

Fill in the book information.

Title:

Author:

Illustrator:

Answer the question.

Have you ever had a fight with a friend? How did it make you feel?

_____

_____

_____

_____

_____

ARNOLD AND LOUISE: LOST AND FOUND (A)

Spelling List 3

Cut out the headings and spelling words. Lay out the headings. Then sort the words by their sound and spelling pattern. After sorting, keep your cutouts in a safe place.

/ŏ/ box	home
/ō/ bone	hop
oddball	hope
both	nod
close	off
come	rock
cone	spot

Think About Reading:
Arnold and Louise: Lost and Found (B)

Answer the question before reading Chapters Two and Three of *Arnold and Louise: Lost and Found.*

1. What do you predict will happen with Arnold and Louise in Chapters Two and Three?

_____

_____

_____

Answer the question after reading Chapters Two and Three of *Arnold and Louise: Lost and Found.*

2. Did your prediction happen? If it happened, explain how it happened. If your prediction did not happen, explain what happened instead.

_____

_____

_____

Describe Arnold and Louise

Answer each question. You can use the words in the box to help you, if you wish.

Describing Words

patient	forgetful	active
playful	kind	silly

1. Think about Arnold.

   a. Write a sentence to **describe** Arnold.

   _____

   _____

   b. Use a detail from the story to explain your answer.

   I know this because _____

   _____

2. Think about Louise.

    a. Write a sentence to **describe** Louise.

    _____

    _____

    b. Use a detail from the story to explain your answer.

    I know this because _____

    _____

    _____

Practice: Spelling List 3

Get your spelling cutouts. Set up the headings, and sort the spelling words again.

Look at your sort, and write down each spelling word under the correct heading on the chart.

/ŏ/ box	/ō/ bone	oddball

Do one of the following activities to practice your spelling words:

Write sentences.

Choose four of your spelling words. Write a sentence using each word.

Write part of a story.

Choose four of your spelling words. Write part of a story using the four words.

Think About Reading:
Arnold and Louise: Lost and Found (C)

Answer the question before reading Chapter Four
of *Arnold and Louise: Lost and Found.*

1. What do you predict will happen with Arnold and
    Louise in Chapter Four?

    _____

    _____

    _____

Answer the question after reading Chapter Four of
Arnold and Louise: Lost and Found.

2. Did your prediction happen? If it happened,
    explain how it happened. If your prediction did
    not happen, explain what happened instead.

    _____

    _____

    _____

Apply: Spelling List 3

Answer the question.

1. What have you learned about words like *box* and
   bone that have the vowel *o*?

   _____

   _____

   _____

   _____

Build new words with the sounds /ŏ/ and /ō/.
The first ones have been done for you.

2. Use the letters in the box to fill in the blanks and
build new words. You may use each letter more
than once.

d h l p r s t

s h o p _____   _____ r o p e

_____ o _____   _____ o _____ e

_____ o _____   _____ o _____ e

_____ o _____   _____ o _____ e

_____ o _____   _____ o _____ e

ARNOLD AND LOUISE: LOST AND FOUND (C)

Think About Reading:
Arnold and Louise: Lost and Found (D)

Answer the question before reading Chapter Five of *Arnold and Louise: Lost and Found.*

1. What do you predict will happen with Arnold and Louise in Chapter Five?

_____

_____

_____

Answer the question after reading Chapter Five of *Arnold and Louise: Lost and Found.*

2. Did your prediction happen? If it happened, explain how it happened. If your prediction did not happen, explain what happened instead.

_____

_____

_____

Use an Irregular Plural Noun

A **noun** shows a person, place, or thing.

A **singular noun** shows *one* person, place, or thing.
A **plural noun** shows *more than one*.

An **irregular plural noun** has a special spelling.

Circle the word that correctly completes each sentence.

1. There are two (childs/children) in my family.

2. Lexi drew a picture of four (mice/mouses).

3. Some (gooses/geese) just flew over the building.

4. There was only one (man/men) at the store.

5. How many (feet/foots) tall is the tree?

For each singular noun,

• Form the plural noun.

• Use the plural noun in a sentence.

• Read the sentence aloud.

6. tooth

    a. plural: _____

    b. sentence:

    _____

    _____

7. fish

    a. plural: _____

    b. sentence:

    _____

    _____

Think About Reading: "Bears in Danger" (A)

Answer Questions 1 and 2 before reading the article "Bears in Danger."

1. What do you know about bears?

_____

_____

_____

2. What is one thing you predict the article will tell you about bears?

_____

_____

_____

Answer Questions 3 and 4 after reading "Bears in Danger."

3. Was your prediction in the article? Circle one:

   Yes   No

4. If your prediction was in the article, what did the text say that confirmed your prediction? If your prediction was **not** in the article, what did the text say instead?

   _____

   _____

   _____

I can't bear waiting to confirm my prediction!

Spelling List 4

Cut out the headings and spelling words. Lay out the headings. Then sort the words by their sound and spelling pattern. After sorting, keep your cutouts in a safe place.

/ŭ/ *bus*	huge
/ū/ *cube*	hunt
oddball	much
cub	mule
cute	pull
does	sun
fume	us

Compare and Contrast Bears

Use the article "Bears in Danger" to find information to complete each sentence.

1. Polar bears are different from giant pandas.

   Polar bears live _____.

   Giant pandas live _____.

2. Sun bears and sloth bears are the same because

   some people capture _____.

3. Sun bears and Andean bears are both in danger

   of losing their homes because _____

   _____.

4. Giant pandas are different from sloth bears.

   Giant pandas eat _____.

   Sloth bears eat _____.

Practice: Spelling List 4

Get your spelling cutouts. Set up the headings, and sort the spelling words again.

Look at your sort, and write down each spelling word under the correct heading on the chart.

/ŭ/ bus	/ū/ cube	oddball

Do one of the following activities to practice your spelling words:

Draw and label.

Choose four of your spelling words. Draw a picture for each word. Then write the word under the picture.

Create a comic strip.

Create four panels of a comic strip. Draw pictures and write text with four or more of your spelling words.

"BEARS IN DANGER" (B)

Model Paragraph

Read the model. Use it to help you as you work on your own paragraph.

Animal Homes

topic sentence

There are many kinds of animal homes. Animals live in trees or inside caves. Other animals live below the ground in burrows. They can even make burrows under the snow. Some animals live in water. A snail's home is its shell. It carries the shell around on its back. Animal homes are not all the same.

supporting details

concluding sentence

Plan Your Paragraph

Read the writing prompt.

Prompt: Write a paragraph about something you know a lot about.

Follow the instructions to brainstorm a topic.

1. What do you know a lot about? List your ideas.

   _____   _____

   _____   _____

   _____   _____

2. Pick one topic that you listed. If you need to, make your topic smaller.

   Big topic: animals

   Smaller topic: animal homes

   My topic is _____ .

Fill out the chart to plan your paragraph.

Main Idea

Supporting Detail

Supporting Detail

Supporting Detail

"BEARS IN DANGER" (C)

Apply: Spelling List 4

Answer the question. Then complete the chart.

1. What have you learned about the sounds and spelling patterns for the vowel *u*?

_____

_____

_____

2. Write each word where it goes in the chart.

cut   from   mute   up   use

/ŭ/ *bus*	/ū/ *cube*	oddball

"BEARS IN DANGER" (C)

Draft Your Paragraph

Write the first draft of your paragraph. Write only on the white rows. You will use the purple rows later.

Title: _____

start here ▶

keep writing ▶

Revise and Proofread Your Paragraph

Use the checklists. Make changes on the purple lines of your draft.

Revising

☐ My topic sentence states my main idea.

☐ My details support my main idea.

☐ My concluding sentence sums up the paragraph.

Proofreading

☐ My sentences are complete.

☐ My sentences start with a capital letter.

☐ My sentences end with an end mark.

☐ I spelled all my words correctly.

Spelling List 5

Cut out the headings and spelling words. Lay out the headings. Then sort the words by their sound and spelling pattern. After sorting, keep your cutouts in a safe place.

–k *book*	look
–ck *duck*	luck
–ke *bike*	snack
broke	snake
brook	speak
cheek	spike
knock	woke
lick	

Think About Reading:
Goldilocks (A)

Fill in the book information.

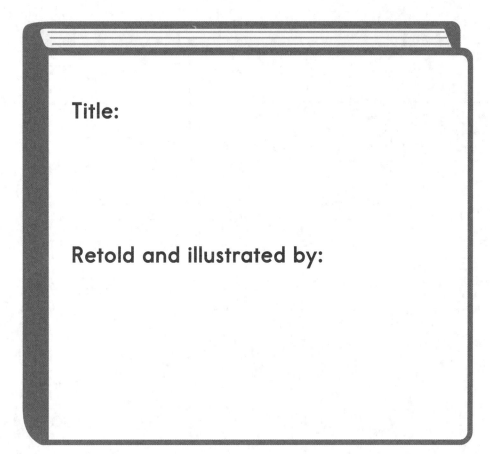

Title:

Retold and illustrated by:

Answer the question.

Do you think that it's OK for a person to go into somebody else's home without asking first? Why or why not?

_____

_____

_____

_____

Publish Your Paragraph

Write a clean copy of your paragraph.

_____

_____

_____

_____

_____

_____

_____

_____

Practice: Spelling List 5

Get your spelling cutouts. Set up the headings, and sort the spelling words again.

Look at your sort, and write down each spelling word under the correct heading on the chart.

–k *book*	–ck *duck*	–ke *bike*

Do one of the following activities to practice your spelling words:

Write sentences.

Choose four of your spelling words. Write a sentence using each word.

Write part of a story.

Choose four of your spelling words. Write part of a story using the four words.

_____

_____

_____

_____

_____

_____

Apply: Spelling List 5

Answer the question.

1. What have you learned about words that end with the sound /k/?

_____

_____

_____

Do the word hunt.

2. Circle words that end with the patterns –k, –ck, and –ke.

> Today, I went for a hike along a creek. When I hike, I like to look for interesting things. This time, I found a rock shaped like a duck. It was huge, so I couldn't take it home with me. Instead, I set down my pack and took a break on the rock. Then I saw a big black cloud. A storm was coming. So, I headed back home.

Spelling List 6

Cut out the headings and spelling words. Lay out the headings. Then sort the words by their sound and spelling pattern. After sorting, keep your cutouts in a safe place.

–nd	pretend
–nk	second
–nt	stink
around	think
front	went
grunt	wind
junk	yank
mount	

Use an Irregular Past Tense Verb

A **verb** shows an action or links ideas.

A verb in the **past tense** shows an action that already happened.

An **irregular past tense verb** has a special spelling.

Circle the word that correctly completes each sentence.

1. Neel (sitted/sat) in the chair.

2. Eva (grew/growed) two inches this year.

3. Yesterday, we (ate/eated) a treat.

4. The children (swimmed/swam) on the hot day.

5. I (writed/wrote) a poem about my family.

For each verb,

• Form the past tense.

• Use the past tense in a sentence.

• Read the sentence aloud.

6. hide

    a. past tense: _____

    b. sentence:

    _____

    _____

7. tell

    a. past tense: _____

    b. sentence:

    _____

    _____

Practice: Spelling List 6

Get your spelling cutouts. Set up the headings, and sort the spelling words again.

Look at your sort, and write down each spelling word under the correct heading on the chart.

–nd	–nk	–nt

Do one of the following activities to practice your spelling words:

Draw and label.

Choose four of your spelling words. Draw a picture for each word. Then write the word under the picture.

Create a comic strip.

Create four panels of a comic strip. Draw pictures and write text with four or more of your spelling words.

Comparing Goldilocks Stories

Answer the questions in the chart to compare
Goatilocks and the Three Bears to *Brownilocks and
the Three Bowls of Cornflakes.*

Question	Goatilocks	Brownilocks
Who is the main character?		
Whose home does the main character go into?		
What does the main character eat in the home?		
What does the main character do at the end of the story? Why does she do that?		

Apply: Spelling List 6

Answer the question.

1. What have you learned about the spelling patterns *–nd*, *–nk*, and *–nt?*

_____

_____

_____

_____

**Build new words with the endings _-nd_, _-nk_, and _-nt_.
The first ones have been done for you.**

2. Use the letters in the box to fill in the blanks and
build new words. You may use each letter more
than once.

```
a   e   i   b   l   s   t
```

s a	nd	b l i	nk	t e	nt
	nd		nk		nt
	nd		nk		nt
	nd		nk		nt

Theme Time: Bears

You have read about make-believe bears and real bears. Many of the bears had a problem. Answer the questions.

1. What is one of Arnold's problems in *Arnold and Louise: Lost and Found*?

_____

_____

_____

2. According to the article "Bears in Danger," polar bears are facing a problem. What is that problem?

_____

_____

_____

3. In *Goatilocks and the Three Bears*, what problem does the family of bears have?

_____

_____

_____

(Optional) Complete the mini-project.

Use puppets to retell a story.

Instructions:

1. Decide which story you will retell: Goldilocks or Goatilocks.

2. Draw pictures of the three bears and either Goldilocks or Goatilocks.

3. Cut out the pictures. Glue each on to a craft stick to make it into a puppet.

4. Use the puppets to retell the story you chose.

Go Write! and Set a Goal

Respond to the prompt. Or, write about a topic of your choice!

Prompt: Think back to what you learned in the unit. What would you like to learn more about? Why?

My Journal

BEARS WRAP-UP (B)

A goal is something that you want to do.

You are getting ready to start a new unit. Choose one goal for yourself as a reader or writer. Or, write your own goal.

My GOAL!

☐ Read each book twice.

☐ Read for 10 minutes a day.

☐ Read to someone in my family.

☐ Write a paragraph on my own.

☐ _____

_____

Write one thing you can do to help reach your goal.

I will _____

_____

Think About Reading: *Brontorina* (A)

Fill in the book information.

Title:

Author:

Illustrator:

Answer the question before reading *Brontorina*.

1. What do you predict the book *Brontorina* will be about?

   _____

   _____

   _____

   _____

Answer the question after reading *Brontorina*.

2. Did your prediction happen? If it happened, explain how it happened. If your prediction did not happen, explain what happened instead.

   _____

   _____

   _____

   _____

BRONTORINA (A)

Use *And, Or, But*

We use *and, or,* and *but* to join ideas. These words are called **conjunctions**.

Think about the book *Brontorina*. Use *and, or,* or *but* to complete each sentence.

1. Brontorina wants to dance _____ does not have the right shoes.

2. Clara _____ Jack are kind to Brontorina.

3. Do you think Brontorina would like hip-hop _____ salsa dancing better?

Use the mentor sentence. Replace the missing words with your own words.

4. **Mentor sentence:** Brontorina is gigantic but very graceful.

   My sentence: I am _____ but

   _____ .

5. Mentor sentence: The new dance academy has space for everyone and shoes of all sizes.

   My sentence: My favorite place has _____

   _____ and _____ .

6. Mentor sentence: Children or animals can dance at the new academy.

   My sentence: _____ or _____

   can _____ .

Choose one sentence that you wrote. Rearrange the sentence in a new way that still makes sense. You can add or remove words if you need to.

Example for Mentor Sentence 6: At the new academy, animals or children can dance.

I chose Sentence _____ .

My new sentence: _____

_____

Spelling List 7

Cut out the headings and spelling words. Lay out the headings. Then sort the words by their sound and spelling pattern. After sorting, keep your cutouts in a safe place.

īCC *mind*	y *fly*
igh *high*	oddball
buy	might
child	right
dry	sigh
fight	spy
find	why
kind	wild

Solve a Problem

Answer the questions.

1. One of the problems in the book *Brontorina* is that Brontorina is too big to fit in Madame Lucille's dance studio. How is the problem solved in the story?

_____

_____

_____

2. How would you have solved the problem?

_____

_____

_____

3. Draw a picture that shows how you would solve the problem.

Practice: Spelling List 7

Get your spelling cutouts. Set up the headings, and sort the spelling words again.

Look at your sort, and write down each spelling word under the correct heading on the chart.

īCC *mind*	igh *high*	y *fly*	oddball

Do one of the following activities to practice your spelling words:

Write sentences.

Choose four of your spelling words. Write a sentence using each word.

Write part of a story.

Choose four of your spelling words. Write part of a story using the four words.

BRONTORINA (B)

Think About Reading:
If the Dinosaurs Came Back (A)

Fill in the book information.

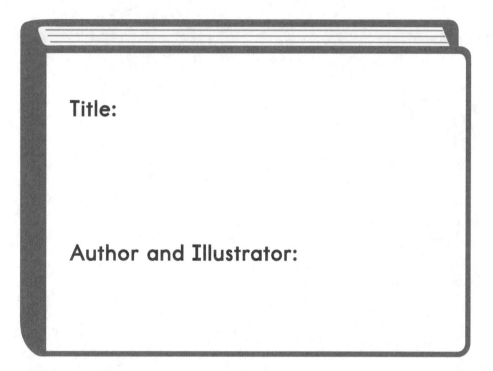

Title:

Author and Illustrator:

Answer the question.

What do you think would happen if the dinosaurs came back?

_____

_____

_____

What If?

We can start a sentence with *if*. Most sentences that start with *if* have two complete thoughts. A comma comes after the first thought.

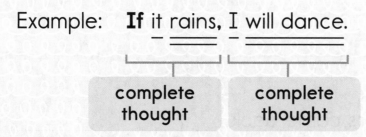

Example: **If** it rains, I will dance.

| complete thought | complete thought |

Read each sentence from *If the Dinosaurs Came Back* aloud.

• **Underline each complete thought.**

• **Circle the comma.**

1. If the dinosaurs came back, we wouldn't need any more lawn mowers.

2. If the dinosaurs came back, they could help build big skyscrapers.

What do you think would happen if the dinosaurs came back? Complete each sentence. Don't forget the comma!

3. If the dinosaurs came back __ _____

_____

_____

4. If the dinosaurs came back __ _____

_____

_____

Write your own sentence that starts with "if" and has two complete thoughts. Don't forget the comma!

5. If _____ __

                complete thought

_____

                complete thought

IF THE DINOSAURS CAME BACK (A)

Choose a starter word from the box. Write a sentence that starts with the word and has two complete thoughts. Don't forget the comma!

Starter Words

After   Before   Though   When

6. _____   _____   ____
   starter word   complete thought

   _____
                      complete thought

Apply: Spelling List 7

Answer the question. Then complete the chart.

1. What have you learned about the spelling patterns for the long i sound, /ī/?

_____

_____

_____

2. Write each word where it goes in the chart.

> cry   mild   night   pie   sight   sky

īCC *mind*	igh *high*	y *fly*	oddball

IF THE DINOSAURS CAME BACK (A)

A Dinosaur's Perspective

Answer the question and draw a picture.

1. Imagine you are a dinosaur. How would you feel about helping people in the ways the story describes?

_____

_____

_____

_____

Imagine?
But, I *am* a dinosaur!

2. Draw a picture that shows a way dinosaurs could help people. Use thought bubbles to show what the dinosaurs think about helping.

IF THE DINOSAURS CAME BACK (B)

More Practice: Spelling List 7

Get your spelling cutouts. Do not use the heading cutouts.

Pile the cutouts face down. Turn over one cutout at a time, and then write the spelling word under the correct heading.

īCC *mind*	igh *high*	y *fly*	oddball

Think About Reading:
Truth or Lie: Dinosaurs! (A)

Answer the questions before you read *Truth or Lie: Dinosaurs!*

1. What is the topic of the book *Truth or Lie: Dinosaurs!*?

   _____

2. What do you know about the topic of *Truth or Lie: Dinosaurs!*?

   _____

   _____

   _____

   _____

   _____

Answer the question after you read *Truth or Lie: Dinosaurs!*

3. What are two facts that you learned about dinosaurs from the book *Truth or Lie: Dinosaurs!*?

_____

_____

_____

_____

_____

_____

TRUTH OR LIE: DINOSAURS! (A)

Model Three Truths and a Lie

Read the model. Use it to help you as you work on your own short research assignment.

Truth or Lie: Jellyfish!

fact from research
1. Jellyfish can be as large as six feet across.

lie
2. Jellyfish can easily escape predators.

fact from research
3. Jellyfish can live in the sand.

fact from research
4. Some jellyfish live cold water, and some live in warm water.

why the lie is a lie
The lie is number 2. Jellyfish drift slowly in big groups. They are an easy meal for predators!

My Research Source

Title: Jellyfish

Author: Valerie Bodden

My Animal Research

Write the title and author of your research source.
Then write four facts you found in that book.

Fact:

_____

_____

_____

_____

Page: _____

Fact:

_____

_____

_____

_____

Page: _____

My Research Source

Title: _____

_____

Author: _____

Fact:

_____

_____

_____

Page: _____

Fact:

_____

_____

_____

Page: _____

Write ideas for a lie about your animal.

Lie:

_____

_____

_____

Lie:

_____

_____

_____

Lie:

_____

_____

_____

TRUTH OR LIE: DINOSAURS! (A)

Spelling List 8

Cut out the headings and spelling words. Lay out the headings. Then sort the words by their sound and spelling pattern. After sorting, keep your cutouts in a safe place.

/ĕ/ bed	/ē/ eat
/ē/ feet	oddball
been	meat
best	meet
check	pea
feather	read
green	sleep
mean	teeth

Draft Your Three Truths and a Lie

Write the first draft of your three truths and a lie.

☐ Choose three facts from your research.
 Write them in your own words.

☐ Write one lie about your animal.

☐ Write which statement is a lie, and explain why.

Write only on the white rows. You will use the purple rows later.

Title: Truth or Lie: _____ !

start here ▶

keep writing ▶

keep writing ▶

TRUTH OR LIE: DINOSAURS! (C)

keep writing ▶

TRUTH OR LIE: DINOSAURS! (C)

Practice: Spelling List 8

Get your spelling cutouts. Set up the headings, and sort the spelling words again.

Look at your sort, and write down each spelling word under the correct heading on the chart.

/ĕ/ bed	/ē/ feet	/ē/ eat	oddball

Do one of the following activities to practice your spelling words:

Draw and label.

Choose four of your spelling words. Draw a picture for each word. Then write the word under the picture.

Create a comic strip.

Create four panels of a comic strip. Draw pictures and write text with four or more of your spelling words.

Revise and Proofread Your Three Truths and a Lie

Use the revising checklist. Make changes on the purple lines of your draft.

Revising

☐ I wrote three facts and one lie.

☐ I identified the lie.

☐ I explained why the lie is a lie.

☐ My facts are in my own words.

☐ My facts are true.

Find at least three words in your draft that you think may be misspelled. Use a dictionary to check each spelling. Correct any misspelled words on the purple lines of your draft.

Word in my draft: _____

Dictionary spelling: _____

Word in my draft: _____

Dictionary spelling: _____

Word in my draft: _____

Dictionary spelling: _____

Use the proofreading checklist. Make changes on the purple lines of your draft.

Proofreading

☐ My sentences are complete.

☐ My sentences start with a capital letter.

☐ My sentences end with an end mark.

☐ I used the words *and*, *or*, and *but* correctly to connect ideas.

☐ I spelled all my words correctly.

Apply: Spelling List 8

Answer the question.

1. What have you learned about the spelling patterns for the sounds /ĕ/ and /ē/?

_____

_____

_____

Build new words with the sounds /ĕ/ and /ē/.
The first ones have been done for you.

2. Use the letters in the box to fill in the blanks and
   build new words. You may use each letter more
   than once.

b   d   f   m   s   t

__s__ e __t__   __t__ ea____   __f__ ee __t__

____ e ____   ____ ea ____   ____ ee ____

____ e ____   ____ ea ____   ____ ee ____

____ e ____   ____ ea ____   ____ ee ____

DIGGING INTO DINOSAURS (A)

Publish Your Three Truths and a Lie

Write a clean copy of your three truths and a lie.
At the end, write the title and author of your
research source.

Title: Truth or Lie: _____ !

_____

_____

_____

_____

_____

_____

_____

_____

_____

_____

_____

_____

_____

_____

_____

_____

_____

My Research Source

Title: _____

Author: _____

(Optional) Draw a funny picture to go with your lie.

DIGGING INTO DINOSAURS (B)

More Practice: Spelling List 8

Get your spelling cutouts. Do not use the heading cutouts.

Pile the cutouts face down. Turn over one cutout at a time, and then write the spelling word under the correct heading.

/ĕ/ bed	/ē/ feet	/ē/ eat	oddball

Theme Time: Dinosaurs

You have read fiction and nonfiction books in this unit. Answer the questions.

1. Which two books in this unit are fiction?

_____

_____

2. How do you know that those books are fiction?

_____

_____

_____

3. How do you know the book *Truth or Lie: Dinosaurs!* is nonfiction?

_____

_____

_____

(Optional) Complete the mini-project.

Brontorina's dream was to be a dancer. What is something you dream of becoming?

Instructions:

1. Draw and color a picture that shows something you dream of becoming.

2. Write one or more sentences that tell what you dream of becoming and why that is your dream.

Go Write! and Set a Goal

Respond to the prompt. Or, write about a topic of your choice!

Prompt: Imagine you had a pet dinosaur. Write about the things you and your dinosaur would do together.

My Journal

A goal is something that you want to do.

You are getting ready to start a new unit. Choose one goal for yourself as a reader or writer. Or, write your own goal.

My GOAL!

☐ Read each book twice.

☐ Read for 10 minutes a day.

☐ Read to someone in my family.

☐ Research something on my own.

☐ _____

_____

Write one thing you can do to help reach your goal.

I will _____

_____

Think About Reading: "The Life of a Butterfly" (A)

Answer the question and draw a picture.

1. What do you know about butterflies?

_____

_____

_____

2. Draw a picture of a butterfly.

Reflect: "The Life of a Butterfly" (A)

Read the excerpt from "The Life of a Butterfly."

> Finally, the chrysalis cracks open. What comes out? It is not a squirmy caterpillar. It is not a pupa. It is a butterfly with beautiful colored wings!

Follow the steps to make inferences. The first one has been done for you.

1. What inference can you make about a caterpillar?

   a. What I read: A caterpillar does not come out of the chrysalis.

   b. What I know: I only see caterpillars in the springtime.

   c. I can infer that a caterpillar does not live very long.

2. What inference can you make about a butterfly?

  a. What I read:

  _____

  _____

  b. What I know:

  _____

  _____

  _____

  c. I can infer that a butterfly

  _____

  _____

  _____

"THE LIFE OF A BUTTERFLY" (A)

Spelling List 9

Cut out the headings and spelling words. Lay out the headings. Then sort the words by their sound and spelling pattern. After sorting, keep your cutouts in a safe place.

oCe *bone*	ow *snow*
oa *coat*	oddball
float	nose
goes	show
grow	those
know	toast
load	whole
move	yellow

It's All in the Details

Write a paragraph about your favorite thing to do.

_____

_____

_____

_____

_____

_____

_____

_____

Circle the main idea of your paragraph.

Underline two details that support the main idea.

Practice: Spelling List 9

Get your spelling cutouts. Set up the headings, and sort the spelling words again.

Look at your sort, and write down each spelling word under the correct heading on the chart.

oCe *bone*	oa *coat*	ow *snow*	oddball

Do one of the following activities to practice your spelling words:

Write sentences.

Choose four of your spelling words. Write a sentence using each word.

Write part of a story.

Choose four of your spelling words. Write part of a story using the four words.

_____

_____

_____

_____

_____

_____

_____

Use a Reflexive Pronoun

A **reflexive pronoun** names someone who has already been named in the sentence.

Example: Anna poured **herself** a cup of water.

A reflexive pronoun ends in *–self* or *–selves*.

Singular	Plural
myself, yourself, himself, herself, itself	ourselves, yourselves, themselves

Complete each sentence with the correct reflexive pronoun.

1. Jamie and Dee planted the flowers _____ .

2. Did you rake those leaves by _____ , Manny?

3. We made breakfast _____ today.

4. The ant moved that huge leaf by _____ !

Use the mentor sentence.

• Replace the missing words with your own words.

• Read your sentence aloud.

5. **Mentor sentence:** I used to need help brushing my teeth, but now I can do that by myself.

   My sentence: I used to need help _____

   _____ , but now I can do that by myself.

6. **Mentor sentence:** Jerome built himself a fort out of sticks.

   My sentence: _____ built _____

   a fort out of sticks.

Write a sentence using the reflexive pronoun *yourselves*.

7. **My sentence:** _____

   _____

   _____

"THE LIFE OF A BUTTERFLY" (C)

Apply: Spelling List 9

Answer the question.

1. What have you learned about words like *nose*,
   float, and *snow* that have the vowel *o*?

_____

_____

_____

_____

Build new words with the sound /ō/. The first ones have been done for you.

2. Use the letters in the box to fill in the blanks and build new words. You may use each letter more than once.

b g d h p r s t

p o s e   b oa s t   t h r ow

_ o _ e   _ oa _   _ ow

_ o _ e   _ oa _   _ ow

_ o _ e   _ oa _   _ ow

Think About Reading: *Praying Mantis* (A)

Fill in the book information.

Title:

Author:

Answer the question and draw a picture.

1. What do you know about praying mantises?

_____

_____

2. Draw a picture of a praying mantis.

PRAYING MANTIS (A)

Reflect: *Praying Mantis* (A)

Read the excerpt from *Praying Mantis.*

> When autumn begins, the female praying mantis lays her eggs….She covers the eggs in a liquid that hardens. This keeps the eggs safe from hungry creatures and harsh winter weather.

Answer the questions.

1. What inference can you make about a praying mantis's eggs?

   a. What I read:

   _____

   _____

   b. What I know:

   _____

   _____

c. I can infer that a praying mantis

_____

_____

2. What did you learn about a praying mantis?

_____

_____

_____

_____

Make the Subject and Verb Agree

A subject and a verb must agree.

- We use a **singular verb** with a singular subject.

    Example: The ant climbs the tree trunk.

- We use a **plural verb** with a plural subject. We also use a plural verb with the pronouns *I* and *you*.

    Examples: Leaves blow in the wind.

    I see the leaves.

Circle the word that correctly completes each sentence.

1. The praying mantis (grabs/grab) its prey.

2. Spiders (eats/eat) praying mantises.

3. You really (likes/like) reading about insects!

4. That nymph in the leaves (looks/look) like a small adult mantis.

Complete each sentence. Use one of the verbs in the box. Use a punctuation mark.

Verbs

walk	bake	grow	clap	love
walks	bakes	grows	claps	loves

5. I _____

_____

6. My friend _____

_____

More Practice: Spelling List 9

Get your spelling cutouts. Do not use the heading cutouts.

Pile the cutouts face down. Turn over one cutout at a time, and then write the spelling word under the correct heading.

oCe *bone*	oa *coat*	ow *snow*	oddball

Any Questions?

Read the excerpt from *Praying Mantis*. Then write one question you have about the text.

1.

> Praying mantises look very strange. The largest can reach the size of a small bird. They can stand on their back legs. They hold their front legs as if they are praying. That is how they got their name.

Example question: How small can a praying mantis be?

My question:

_____

_____

2.

The long front legs of the mantis may make it look like it is praying. But it is really waiting for a snack to wander by. Then it grabs its prey with its front legs. The tiny spikes on those legs hold its prey in place.

My question:

_____

_____

3.

The mantis uses its legs for walking, climbing, jumping, and hunting. It also has two pairs of wings. It uses them to get away from predators. A mantis being chased by a bat will fly up and down, left and right to escape.

My question:

_____

_____

Think About Reading: "Honey from the Hive" (A)

Answer the question before reading
"Honey from the Hive."

1. How do you think bees make honey?

_____

_____

_____

_____

Answer the questions after reading
"Honey from the Hive."

2. How was your prediction similar to the steps in
the article?

_____

_____

_____

3. How was your prediction different from the steps in the article?

_____

_____

_____

_____

"HONEY FROM THE HIVE" (A)

Draw a Cartoon Bee

Listen to the directions online.

1. Restate the directions aloud in your own words.

2. Follow the directions to finish drawing the bee.

3. Give someone directions for how to color the bee. Use three steps. You can plan your directions here.

1. _____

2. _____

3. _____

"HONEY FROM THE HIVE" (A)

Spelling List 10

Cut out the headings and spelling words. Lay out the headings. Then sort the words by their sound and spelling pattern. After sorting, keep your cutouts in a safe place.

uCe *tube*	ue *blue*
ew *flew*	oo *moon*
clue	knew
dew	new
due	rule
pool	true
glue	tune
June	boot

Model How-To

Read the model. Use it to help you as you work on your own how-to.

A Perfect Sandwich

topic sentences

> Do you want to make a quick, delicious, and healthy lunch? If so, peanut butter and jelly is the perfect sandwich for you!

steps

> First, get two pieces of bread, peanut butter, and jelly. Next, use a knife to carefully spread peanut butter on one side of one piece of bread. After that, use a new knife to spread jelly on one side of the other piece. Finally, put the peanut-butter side and the jelly side together to make a sandwich. That's all it takes to make an easy, yummy, nutritious lunch!

concluding sentence

Choose a Topic for Your How-To

Read the writing prompt.

Prompt: **What do you know how to do or make?**
Write a how-to for that process.

Follow the instructions to brainstorm a topic.

1. What do you know well that follows steps?
   List your ideas.

   _____   _____

   _____   _____

   _____   _____

2. Pick one topic that you listed. If you need to,
   make your topic smaller.

   Big topic: how to cook

   Smaller topic: how to make a peanut butter and
   jelly sandwich

   My topic is _____ .

Practice: Spelling List 10

Get your spelling cutouts. Set up the headings, and sort the spelling words again.

Look at your sort, and write down each spelling word under the correct heading on the chart.

uCe *tube*	ew *flew*	ue *blue*	oo *moon*

Do one of the following activities to practice your spelling words:

Draw and label.

Choose four of your spelling words. Draw a picture for each word. Then write the word under the picture.

Create a comic strip.

Create four panels of a comic strip. Draw pictures and write text with four or more of your spelling words.

Think About Reading: "I See a Honeybee" (A)

Answer the question and draw a picture before reading "I See a Honeybee."

1. Honeybees make honey. What else do you know about bees?

_____

_____

_____

_____

2. Draw a picture of a honeybee at work.

Answer the question after reading "I See a Honeybee."

3. What did you learn about honeybees?

_____

_____

_____

_____

_____

_____

"I SEE A HONEYBEE" (A)

Plan Your How-To

Fill out the chart to plan your how-to. You can use words, pictures, or both.

Topic Sentence

Tell what you are showing how to make or do.

Steps

First,

Next,

Last,

↓

Concluding Sentence

Share a final thought.

"I SEE A HONEYBEE" (A)

Apply: Spelling List 10

Answer the question. Then complete the chart.

1. What have you learned about the sound and spelling patterns for the sound long double o, /o͞o/?

    _____

    _____

    _____

2. Write each word where it goes in the chart.

chew   sue   drew   duke   rude   hoop

uCe *tube*	ew *flew*	ue *blue*	oo *moon*

"I SEE A HONEYBEE" (A)

Write Your How-To

Write your how-to as a paragraph. Include
these parts:

☐ Title

☐ Topic sentence

☐ Steps that start with order words like
First, *Next*, and *Last*

☐ Concluding sentence

Title: _____

_____

_____

_____

_____

"I SEE A HONEYBEE" (B)

More Practice: Spelling List 10

Get your spelling cutouts. Do not use the heading cutouts.

Pile the cutouts face down. Turn over one cutout at a time, and then write the spelling word under the correct heading.

uCe *tube*	ew *flew*	ue *blue*	oo *moon*

Think About Reading: "The Bee's Knees" (A)

Answer the question before reading
"The Bee's Knees: Insects Are Awesome!"

1. How do insects help people?

_____

_____

_____

_____

_____

_____

Answer the question after reading "The Bee's Knees: Insects Are Awesome!"

2. Think about the ways insects help people. Make an inference.

   Example inference: It is important to save insects.

   _____

   _____

   _____

   _____

   _____

   _____

Write an Opinion Statement

Read the writing prompt.

Prompt: Think about the article "The Bee's Knees: Insects Are Awesome!" and the video about spotted lanternflies. How do YOU feel about insects?

Brainstorm your feelings about insects. Write or draw your ideas in the insect shape.

Write an opinion statement about insects. Use the mentor sentence to help you.

Mentor sentence: We should all protect insects because they do important jobs.

My opinion statement:

_____

_____

_____

"THE BEE'S KNEES: INSECTS ARE AWESOME!" (A)

Support an Opinion

Think about the opinion statement you wrote about insects.

1. Brainstorm facts that support your opinion.

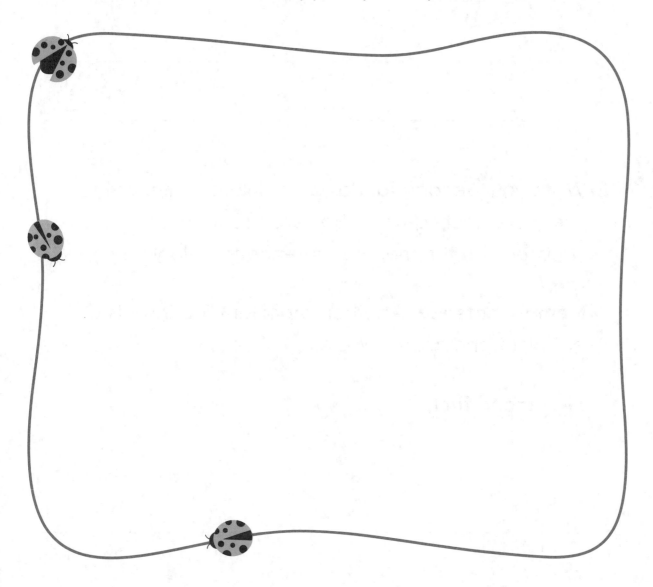

2. Circle your two strongest facts.

3. Write your first fact as a complete sentence.
Use the mentor sentence to help you.

Mentor sentence: First, insects like butterflies
move pollen among flowers.

My first fact:

_____

_____

4. Write your second fact as a complete sentence.
Use a connecting word like _too_, _also_, _and_, or
another. Use the mentor sentence to help you.

Mentor sentence: Another important job insects do is
eat plant and animal waste.

My second fact:

_____

_____

Spelling List 11

Cut out the headings and spelling words. Lay out the headings. Then sort the words by their sound and spelling pattern. After sorting, keep your cutouts in a safe place.

aCe *cake*	ay *day*
ai *rain*	oddball
aid	make
always	paint
away	plane
chase	pray
claim	said
gain	stay

Read: Insect Poetry (A)

Insect

The feelers on an insect's head
help it sense
its world.
Compound eyes
help the insect see
what's wiggling by.
Its mouthparts jab
or suck or chew
food to crunch
for lunch.
The thorax has
two sets of wings a
zinging bug can use.
Six strong legs help it
spring   or   catch,
swim or dig or sing.
The abdomen
is the largest,
full of insect parts.
A shell made
of hard stuff like
fingernails or toenails
keeps the bug in its
topflight shape
from feelers
to
s
t
i
n
g
e
r
.

How Many?

How many insects are in the world?

Guess.

More than pine cones in the trees?

More than worms underground?

More than spiders spinning webs?

Yes.

How many insects are in the world?

Guess.

More than flowers in the fields?

More than salmon in the streams?

More than dolphins swimming seas?

Yes.

How many insects are in the world?

Guess.

More than clovers in the grass?

More than birds skimming skies?

More than people on the earth?

Yes.

Many,

    many,

        more.

Housefly

Got glop, a mess, banana peels?

I'm your guy for slurping slop.

Got slime, old meat, a compost pile?

I'm your guy for greasy grime.

Got goo, potatoes slightly soft?

I'm your guy for stinky stew.

Got waste, bad beans, some smelly fish?

I'm your guy. I like the taste.

Got rot, green cheese, some sour milk?

I'm Housefly. It hits the spot.

Write a Shape Poem

Write your own shape poem. Use sensory details.

Practice: Spelling List 11

Get your spelling cutouts. Set up the headings, and sort the spelling words again.

Look at your sort, and write down each spelling word under the correct heading on the chart.

aCe *cake*	ai *rain*	ay *day*	oddball

Do one of the following activities to practice your spelling words:

Write sentences.

Choose four of your spelling words. Write a sentence using each word.

Write part of a story.

Choose four of your spelling words. Write part of a story using the four words.

_____

_____

_____

_____

_____

_____

Read: Insect Poetry (B)

A Caterpillar's Job

A caterpillar's job
is to hatch from an egg
and grow fast as a flash.

A caterpillar's job
is to gobble and gulp
leaf after juicy leaf.

A caterpillar's job
is to pick a nice stick,
and spin a silky sac.

A caterpillar's job
is to remake itself
into a butterfly.

Pesky Pests

When we think about earth's insects,
we like to call them pests
because they sometimes bother us
with their, often frightening, tricks.

Those same bees, wasps, and mosquitoes,
Who sometimes sting or bite,
make our food as pollinators,
as they flit from plant to plant.

Without certain flies and beetles,
our earth would be a mess.
Chowing down on waste and dead stuff,
they're keeping our world clean.

Icky ticks are food for critters
like lizards, birds, and frogs.
Bats swoop low in the dark of night
for yummy mosquito meals.

So, think of the insects kindly
no matter what they do.
They're not pests but buzzy helpers.
We would sink without their skills.

Apply: Spelling List 11

Answer the question.

1. What have you learned about words with the sound /ā/?

_____

_____

_____

_____

Build new words with the sound /ā/. The first ones have been done for you.

2. Use the letters in the box to fill in the blanks and build new words. You may use each letter more than once.

d l n p r t w

<u>l</u> a n e   w ai t   t r ay

_____ a _____ e   _____ ai _____   _____ ay

_____ a _____ e   _____ ai _____   _____ ay

_____ a _____ e   _____ ai _____   _____ ay

INSECT POETRY (B)

Theme Time: Insects

Think about "The Life of a Butterfly," "Honey from the Hive," and "I See a Honeybee." Then answer the questions about the order of events.

1. You learned that butterflies keep changing. What happens to a butterfly after it hatches from the egg?

_____

_____

_____

2. You learned how bees make honey. What do bees do after they gather the nectar?

_____

_____

_____

3. You learned that worker bees gather pollen.
What happens after the bees land on a flower?

_____

_____

_____

(Optional) Complete the mini-project.

Make a diorama to show different kinds of bees and
the jobs they do.

Instructions:

1. Draw, color, and cut out different kinds of bees:
   queen bee, worker bees, drones. Tape your
   bees to craft sticks or pencils.

2. Draw and color places you find bees: a garden,
   inside the hive, outside the hive. Tape or paste
   these places to a shoe box.

3. Use your bees to show the jobs bees do.

Go Write! and Set a Goal

Respond to the prompt. Or, write about a topic of your choice!

Prompt: Would it be most fun to be a honeybee, a praying mantis, or a butterfly? Why?

My Journal

INSECTS WRAP-UP (B)

A goal is something that you want to do.

You are getting ready to start a new unit. Choose one goal for yourself as a reader or writer. Or, write your own goal.

My GOAL!

- ☐ Read each book twice.
- ☐ Read for 10 minutes a day.
- ☐ Read to someone in my family.
- ☐ Write a paragraph on my own.
- ☐ _____
  _____

Write one thing you can do to help reach your goal.

I will _____
_____

Think About Reading: *A Weed is a Flower* (A)

Fill in the book information.

Title:

Author and Illustrator:

Answer the questions.

1. What is a weed?

_____

_____

2. What is a flower?

3. What does the title *A Weed is a Flower* mean to you?

Draw a picture of a weed or a flower.

Model Book Review

Read the model. Use it to help you as you work on your own book review.

Open Your Eyes and Read a Great Book

I read a great book. It is called Zara's Big Messy Day by Rebekah Borucki. The main characters are Zara, Mama, Sam, and Penelope. Zara is a second grader who likes things to go smoothly. One day at breakfast, her brother Sam knocks over her juice. It makes Zara mad. Mama says to Zara, "Close your eyes. Smell the flowers. Blow out the candles." Mama's words help Zara feel better. Zara uses Mama's words again when Penelope makes fun of her shoes. And, she uses the words one more time when Sam knocks over her tower of blocks. The words help each time. In the end, Zara's day turns out OK.

— summary

This book is great for kids. It can help kids deal with their own feelings. It has already helped me! One day, my brother made me angry. We were playing checkers, and when I was about to win, he quit. I wanted to throw the checkerboard at him. Instead, I closed my eyes and breathed out slowly. Just like Zara, I felt better! I asked my mom to help me talk to my brother. All kids get mad sometimes. By reading Zara's Big Messy Day, we can help ourselves when we are mad. Also, the story is very real. Many kids know what it's like to have a younger sibling. And, many kids have been teased like Zara.

Do you like stories about kids your age? And, do you ever feel angry and want to feel better? If so, pick up a copy of Zara's Big Messy Day. Open your eyes, find a comfy chair, and read a fantastic book!

Choose a Topic for Your Book Review

Read the writing prompt.

Prompt: Write a **book review**. Tell about the book, and give your opinion of it.

Think of two books that you liked. Write one title in each oval. Make a web with things you liked about each book.

Title of first book:

Title of
second book:

Look at your webs. Which book do you want
to review?

Title: _____

Author: _____

250   A WEED IS A FLOWER (A)

Spelling List 12

Cut out the headings and spelling words. Lay out the headings. Then sort the words by their sound and spelling pattern. After sorting, keep your cutouts in a safe place.

bl–	fl–
cl–	pl–
flower	bloom
flood	black
flat	blow
plant	clay
play	clothes
plain	click

Plan Your Summary

Fill out the chart to plan your summary. Write the events of the story in the order they happened.

About the Book

Title:

Author:

Characters:

Setting:

Beginning

Middle

End

Practice: Spelling List 12

Get your spelling cutouts. Set up the headings, and sort the spelling words again.

Look at your sort, and write down each spelling word under the correct heading on the chart.

bl–	cl–	fl–	pl–

Do one of the following activities to practice your spelling words:

Draw and label.

Choose four of your spelling words. Draw a picture for each word. Then write the word under the picture.

Create a comic strip.

Create four panels of a comic strip. Draw pictures and write text with four or more of your spelling words.

Plan Your Opinion Statement and Reasons

Fill out the chart to plan your opinion statement and reasons. Write your opinion about the book. Write two reasons why you feel that way.

Opinion

Reason	Reason

Apply: Spelling List 12

Answer the question.

1. What have you learned about words that begin with the consonant blends *bl–*, *cl–*, *fl–*, and *pl–*?

_____

_____

_____

_____

Do the word hunt.

2. Circle words that begin with the consonant blends *bl–*, *cl–*, *fl–*, and *pl–*.

> Please clap for the clown! Clara has blue hair and a red blouse. Watch her flip in the air and flop on the floor. She flaps her arms and flies like a plane. She lands with a plop and blows us a kiss. We plan on watching her again.

Draft Your Book Review

Write the first draft of your book review. Write only
on the white rows. You will use the purple rows later.

Title: _____

start here ▶

keep writing ▶

keep writing ▶

A WEED IS A FLOWER (D)

keep writing ▶

keep writing ▶

A WEED IS A FLOWER (D)

keep writing ▶

A WEED IS A FLOWER (D)

Think About Reading: *The Girl Who Thought in Pictures* (A)

Fill in the book information.

Title:

Author:

Illustrator:

Answer the questions.

1. What are you good at doing?

_____

_____

2. How did you learn to do that?

_____

_____

_____

_____

THE GIRL WHO THOUGHT IN PICTURES (A)

Spelling List 13

Cut out the headings and spelling words. Lay out the headings. Then sort the words by their sound and spelling pattern. After sorting, keep your cutouts in a safe place.

ŏCC	lost
ōCC –ost	moss
ōCC –old	most
cold	odd
cost	post
ghost	soft
gold	told
hold	

Revise Your Book Review

Use the checklist. Make changes on the purple lines of your draft.

Summary

I stated my book's

☐ title   ☐ author

☐ main characters   ☐ setting

☐ I retold the beginning, middle, and end.

☐ I put the events in order.

Opinion

☐ I stated my opinion of the book clearly.

☐ I gave two reasons for my opinion.

continued

Opinion (continued)

☐ My reasons are clear and support my opinion.

☐ I used linking words like *and, also*, and *because* to connect my ideas.

~~~~~~

Conclusion

☐ I restated my opinion in a new way.

Practice: Spelling List 13

Get your spelling cutouts. Set up the headings, and sort the spelling words again.

Look at your sort, and write down each spelling word under the correct heading on the chart.

ŏCC	ōCC –ost	ōCC –old

Do one of the following activities to practice your spelling words:

Write sentences.

Choose four of your spelling words. Write a sentence using each word.

Write part of a story.

Choose four of your spelling words. Write part of a story using the four words.

Proofread Your Book Review

Use the checklist. Make changes on the purple lines of your draft.

- ☐ My sentences are complete.

- ☐ My sentences start with a capital letter.

- ☐ My sentences end with an end mark.

- ☐ My words are strong.

- ☐ I combined sentences when it made sense.

- ☐ I spelled all my words correctly.

Apply: Spelling List 13

Answer the question. Then complete the chart.

1. What have you learned about the vowel sounds and spelling patterns for the vowel *o*?

_____

_____

_____

_____

2. Write each word where it goes in the chart.

> almost   bold   boss   sold   loft

ŏCC	ōCC –ost	ōCC –old

THE GIRL WHO THOUGHT IN PICTURES (C)

Publish Your Book Review

Write a clean copy of your book review.
Include these parts:

☐ Title

☐ Summary

☐ Opinion

☐ Conclusion

Title: _____

_____

_____

_____

_____

_____

THE GIRL WHO THOUGHT IN PICTURES (D)

Think About Reading:
The Fabled Life of Aesop (A)

Fill in the book information.

Title:

Author:

Illustrator:

Answer the question.

Have you ever heard a fable? "The Tortoise and the Hare" is a famous one! Can you name any others?

_____

_____

_____

Spelling List 14

Cut out the headings and spelling words. Lay out the headings. Then sort the words by their sound and spelling pattern. After sorting, keep your cutouts in a safe place.

ar *farm*	air *chair*
are *care*	oddball
argue	share
fair	stair
hair	stare
hard	starve
hare	their
scare	where

Practice: Spelling List 14

Get your spelling cutouts. Set up the headings, and sort the spelling words again.

Look at your sort, and write down each spelling word under the correct heading on the chart.

ar *farm*	are *care*	air *chair*	oddball

Do one of the following activities to practice your spelling words:

Draw and label.

Choose four of your spelling words. Draw a picture for each word. Then write the word under the picture.

Create a comic strip.

Create four panels of a comic strip. Draw pictures and write text with four or more of your spelling words.

Plan Your Book Ad

Read the prompt.

Prompt: Make a **book ad**. Use technology. Include key words from your book review. Add pictures, drawings, or video.

Follow the instructions to plan your book ad.

1. Write your opinion statement from your published book review. (You can use your concluding statement, if you wish.)

My Opinion

_____

_____

2. What words or short phrases from your book review support your opinion? Choose strong words and phrases.

THE FABLED LIFE OF AESOP (C)

3. Write or sketch ideas for pictures you can use in your book ad.

4. I will use this technology to make my ad:

☐   slide template

☐   other digital tool: _____

Apply: Spelling List 14

Answer the question.

1. What have you learned about words with the r-controlled vowel *a*?

_____

_____

_____

_____

Build words with the r-controlled vowel sound.
The first ones have been done for you.

2. Use the letters in the box to fill in the blanks
and build words. You may use each letter more
than once.

```
c   f   h   k   l   p   r   s
```

___c_ ar _____   ___fl_ are   ___l_ air

_____ ar _____   _____ are   _____ air

_____ ar _____   _____ are   _____ air

_____ ar _____   _____ are   _____ air

THE FABLED LIFE OF AESOP (C)

Think About Reading:
The Fabled Life of Aesop (D)

Answer the questions.

Think about how you talk to the grown-ups in your life. Now, think about how you talk to your friends, brothers, sisters, or cousins.

1. How is it different?

_____

_____

2. How is it the same?

_____

_____

More Practice: Spelling List 14

Get your spelling cutouts. Do not use the heading cutouts.

Pile the cutouts face down. Turn over one cutout at a time, and then write the spelling word under the correct heading.

ar *farm*	are *care*	air *chair*	oddball

Theme Time: Interesting People

Think about *A Weed is a Flower*, *The Girl Who Thought in Pictures*, and *The Fabled Life of Aesop*. Answer the questions.

1. You read about George Washington Carver. Write three character traits or details that show what made him interesting.

_____

_____

_____

2. You read about Temple Grandin. Write three character traits or details that show what made her interesting.

_____

_____

_____

3. You read about Aesop. Write three character traits or details that show what made him interesting.

_____

_____

_____

(Optional) Complete the mini-project.

Create a time line about important events in your life.

Instructions:

1. Draw a line for your time line on paper or poster board. Use a ruler.

2. Think of important events in your life. Examples are the birth of a sibling, adopting a pet, and starting school.

3. Write the events in order on your time line. Start with the day you were born. Write the date of each event. You can also add drawings or photos.

Go Write! and Set a Goal

Respond to the prompt. Or, write about a topic of your choice!

Prompt: You get to spend a day with one of these people:

- George Washington Carver

- Temple Grandin

- Aesop

Tell who you would pick and why. Then tell all about your day!

My Journal

INTERESTING PEOPLE WRAP-UP (B)

A goal is something that you want to do.

You are getting ready to start a new unit. Choose one goal for yourself as a reader or writer. Or, write your own goal.

My GOAL!

- ☐ Read each book twice.
- ☐ Read for 10 minutes a day.
- ☐ Give and get feedback on a piece of writing.
- ☐ _____

_____

Write one thing you can do to help reach your goal.

I will _____

_____

INTERESTING PEOPLE WRAP-UP (B)

Adjectives in Action

We use **adjectives** to tell more about nouns.

Examples: I walked in the **tall**, **green** grass.

The grass was **soft**.

For each sentence, circle the adjective. Underline the noun that the adjective tells more about.

1. The grateful dove thanked the ant.

2. Did you see that little ant on the leaf?

3. Those feathers are white.

4. The man had a sharp spear.

Rewrite the sentence with the given adjective. The first one has been done for you.

5. Sentence: The ant ate.
   Adjective: hungry

   New sentence: The hungry ant ate.

6. Sentence: A dove helped.
   Adjective: kind

   New sentence: _____

   _____

7. Sentence: I heard a noise.
   Adjective: loud

   New sentence: _____

   _____

Spelling List 15

Cut out the headings and spelling words. Lay out the headings. Then sort the words by their sound and spelling pattern. After sorting, keep your cutouts in a safe place.

✂

er *her*	**eer** *deer*
ear *hear*	**oddball**
cheer	never
fear	peer
fern	spear
herd	steer
hunter	very
near	year

Add Adjectives

Revise the beginning of "The Tortoise and the Hare."
Fill in each blank with an adjective. Use the
adjectives in the box, or use other adjectives.
Make the fable funny, if you wish!

Adjectives

long	short	quick	clever	shiny	important
old	large	green	goofy	tired	mean

Once a _____ hare was making

fun of a _____ tortoise for being

slow. "It's true, I am slow," said the tortoise, "but I can still

beat you in a _____ race."

As soon as the _____ race

started, the hare shot out of sight. At the halfway point,

he was so far ahead that he decided to lie down and

take a _____ nap.

    Meanwhile, the _____ tortoise

kept walking, slowly and steadily, never stopping.

Answer the questions.

1. How did the adjectives you added change the
beginning of "The Tortoise and the Hare"? Explain.

_____

_____

_____

_____

2. What does the moral of this fable mean to you? Explain with an example.

Moral: Slow and steady wins the race.

_____

_____

_____

_____

_____

_____

_____

_____

_____

Practice: Spelling List 15

Get your spelling cutouts. Set up the headings, and sort the spelling words again.

Look at your sort, and write down each spelling word under the correct heading on the chart.

er *her*	ear *hear*	eer *deer*	oddball

Do one of the following activities to practice your spelling words:

Write sentences.

Choose four of your spelling words. Write a sentence using each word.

Write part of a story.

Choose four of your spelling words. Write part of a story using the four words.

_____

_____

_____

_____

_____

_____

Connect Pictures and Plot

Look at the pictures in "The Tortoise and the Hare."
Answer the questions.

1. The first two pictures show the beginning of
   the race.

   a. Where is the tortoise? Describe what you see.

   _____

   _____

   _____

   b. Why is the hare at the top of the page?

   _____

   _____

   _____

2. The last two pictures show the end of the race. Find the tortoise and the hare. Describe what is happening.

_____

_____

_____

_____

FABLES (C)

Apply: Spelling List 15

Answer the question.

1. What have you learned about the spelling patterns *er*, *ear*, and *eer*?

_____

_____

Do the word hunt.

2. Read the text. Circle words with the spelling patterns you have learned: *er*, *ear*, and *eer*.

> My dad is a farmer, so we live out in the country. I cover 5 miles on my bike to get to school. One day, I was riding to school under clear blue skies. So, it was odd that I could hear thunder. Then I realized it wasn't thunder. It was a herd of cattle running right at me. As they got closer, I pedaled faster. Finally, I had to veer off the road to get out of the way. I almost ended up in the river.

Use Adverbs That Tell How

We use **adverbs** to tell more about verbs. Adverbs can show *how* something happens.

Example: I walked **happily** in the tall, green grass.

For each sentence, circle the adverb. Underline the verb that the adverb tells more about.

1. The fox jumped high.

2. He looked at the grapes greedily.

3. The fox angrily spoke about the grapes.

For each sentence, add an adverb. Use the adverbs in the box, or use other adverbs. Underline the verb that the adverb tells more about.

Adverbs That Tell How

slowly	quickly	cheerfully	bravely
nicely	rudely	quietly	loudly

4. Aman talked _____ to his friend.

5. Emma _____ hikes up the big mountain.

6. Jamie sings the song _____ .

More Practice: Spelling List 15

Get your spelling cutouts. Do not use the heading cutouts.

Pile the cutouts face down. Turn over one cutout at a time, and then write the spelling word under the correct heading.

er *her*	ear *hear*	eer *deer*	oddball

Use Adverbs That Tell When

Adverbs can show *when* something happens.

Examples: **Yesterday**, I walked in the tall, green grass.

I **always** walk in the grass.

Circle the adverb in each sentence.

1. The goose lays an egg daily.

2. Soon, the farmer has many eggs.

3. The farmer never gets another egg.

Look what I found **today**!

Complete the passage so that it makes sense. Fill in each blank with an adverb from the box.

Adverbs That Tell When

earlier	later	now	soon
today	tomorrow		yesterday

_____ , I made a card

for Uncle Ken. _____ , I

put the card in the mail. I hope Uncle Ken gets my

card _____ !

Answer the question.

4. What does the moral of the fable "The Goose and the Golden Egg" mean to you? Explain with an example.

Moral: If you always want more, you'll lose what you have.

_____

_____

_____

_____

_____

_____

_____

_____

Spelling List 16

Cut out the headings and spelling words. Lay out the headings. Then sort the words by their sound and spelling pattern. After sorting, keep your cutouts in a safe place.

ire *fire*	girl
ir *bird*	grill
Cr blends	hire
dirt	shirt
drip	tire
first	trick
friend	wire

Model Descriptive Paragraph

Read the model. Use it to help you as you work on your own descriptive paragraph.

I love when it snows. The snowflakes melt on my tongue. The white snow sparkles brightly. It covers everything like a blanket. I like to jump in the soft, fluffy piles of snow. I roll in the snow until I look like a snowman. I wear my heavy jacket, snow pants, a knit hat, a long, fuzzy scarf, thick rubber boots, and red mittens. I hear the ice cracking under my feet. I love to feel the frozen winter air. I see and hear kids playing joyfully in the snow. When it is time to go inside, I can smell and taste sweet hot cocoa.

Freewrite for Your Descriptive Paragraph

Pick a big topic from the box.

Descriptive Topic Ideas

- ☐ a fun park or playground
- ☐ a pet or an animal you know
- ☐ a place to visit, like the library
- ☐ an object that's special to you
- ☐ a food or special meal
- ☐ something outdoors, like a garden
- ☐ a special stuffed animal
- ☐ a favorite activity

Write a smaller topic that you will write about.

Big topic: a special stuffed animal

Smaller topic: my elephant, Ellie

My smaller topic is _____.

Freewrite about your smaller topic. Use words that help readers see, hear, feel, smell, and taste what you are writing about.

Write without worrying if your writing is "good." Let your ideas flow to the page!

Practice: Spelling List 16

Get your spelling cutouts. Set up the headings, and sort the spelling words again.

Look at your sort, and write down each spelling word under the correct heading on the chart.

ire *fire*	ir *bird*	Cr blends

Do one of the following activities to practice your spelling words:

Draw and label.

Choose four of your spelling words. Draw a picture for each word. Then write the word under the picture.

Create a comic strip.

Create four panels of a comic strip. Draw pictures and write text with four or more of your spelling words.

Plan Your Descriptive Paragraph

Get the Model Descriptive Paragraph.

- On the two blank diagonal lines: Write two more supporting details from the paragraph.

- On the blank horizontal lines: Write words from the paragraph that describe the supporting details.

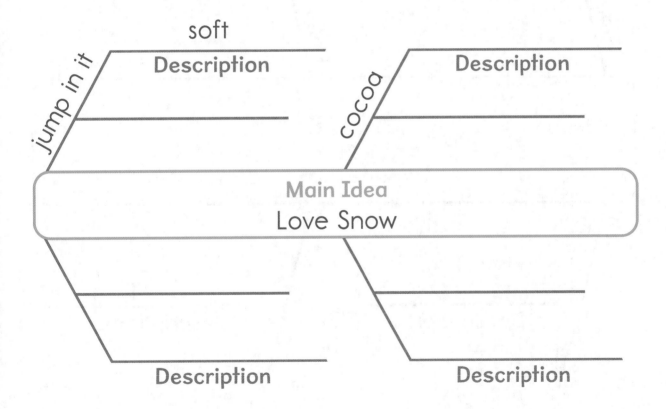

soft

jump in it

Description

cocoa

Description

Main Idea
Love Snow

Description

Description

Use the graphic organizer to plan your descriptive
paragraph. Write your main idea and four details.
Write words to describe each detail. Use ideas from
your freewriting and new ideas, too.

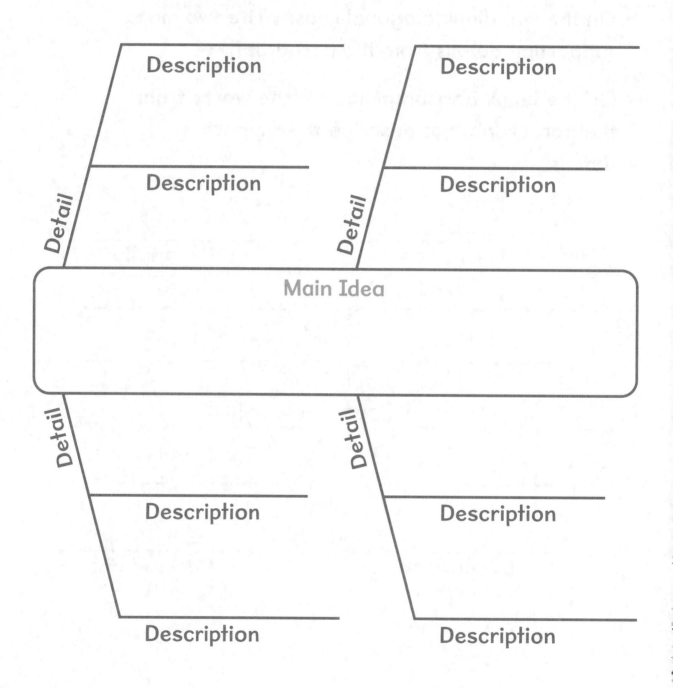

FABLES (H)

Apply: Spelling List 16

Answer the question. Then complete the chart.

1. What have you learned about words with the spelling patterns *ire*, *ir*, and Cr blends?

_____

_____

_____

2. Write each word where it goes in the chart.

crime   mire   third   umpire   bright   firm

ire *fire*	ir *bird*	Cr blends

Fable Questions

Answer the questions.

1. What fable did you choose?

_____

2. Who are the main characters?

_____

_____

3. What is the moral?

_____

_____

4. Write two details from the fable that support
the moral.

_____

_____

_____

Write Your Descriptive Paragraph

Write your descriptive paragraph. Use words that
help readers see, hear, feel, smell, and taste what
you are writing about.

More Practice: Spelling List 16

Get your spelling cutouts. Do not use the heading cutouts.

Pile the cutouts face down. Turn over one cutout at a time, and then write the spelling word under the correct heading.

ire *fire*	ir *bird*	Cr blends

More Fable Questions

Answer the questions.

1. What fable did you choose?

   _____

2. Who are the main characters?

   _____

   _____

3. What is the moral?

   _____

   _____

4. Write two details from the fable that support the moral.

_____

_____

_____

Theme Time: Fables

Think about Aesop's fables. Answer the questions.

1. How do morals help us?

   _____

   _____

   _____

2. Choose a moral from one of the fables you read.
   How does the moral help you in your life?

   _____

   _____

   _____

3. Think about a lesson that is important to you. Write your own moral or change one of Aesop's morals to make it about your life.

_____

_____

_____

(Optional) Complete the mini-project.

Aesop's fables have morals. Do other stories have morals, too?

> **Instructions:**
>
> 1. Choose a book or story you have read.
>
> 2. Think about what lesson you can learn from the story.
>
> 3. Write a moral for the story on construction paper or design it on the computer. Then draw a picture to go with the moral.

Go Write! and Set a Goal

Respond to the prompt. Or, write about a topic of your choice!

Prompt: Pick two characters from the fables you read. Describe what would happen if the characters met. What would they do?

My Journal

FABLES WRAP-UP (B)

A goal is something that you want to do.

You are getting ready to start a new unit. Choose one goal for yourself as a reader or writer. Or, write your own goal.

My GOAL!

☐ Read each book twice.

☐ Read for 10 minutes a day.

☐ Use adjectives and adverbs correctly in my writing.

☐ _____

_____

Write one thing you can do to help reach your goal.

I will _____

_____

My Speed Sort Times

List	Spelling Pattern	First Sort	Second Sort	Third Sort
		_____ min _____ sec	_____ min _____ sec	_____ min _____ sec
		_____ min _____ sec	_____ min _____ sec	_____ min _____ sec
		_____ min _____ sec	_____ min _____ sec	_____ min _____ sec
		_____ min _____ sec	_____ min _____ sec	_____ min _____ sec
		_____ min _____ sec	_____ min _____ sec	_____ min _____ sec
		_____ min _____ sec	_____ min _____ sec	_____ min _____ sec
		_____ min _____ sec	_____ min _____ sec	_____ min _____ sec

List	Spelling Pattern	First Sort	Second Sort	Third Sort
		_____ min _____ sec	_____ min _____ sec	_____ min _____ sec
		_____ min _____ sec	_____ min _____ sec	_____ min _____ sec
		_____ min _____ sec	_____ min _____ sec	_____ min _____ sec
		_____ min _____ sec	_____ min _____ sec	_____ min _____ sec
		_____ min _____ sec	_____ min _____ sec	_____ min _____ sec
		_____ min _____ sec	_____ min _____ sec	_____ min _____ sec
		_____ min _____ sec	_____ min _____ sec	_____ min _____ sec
		_____ min _____ sec	_____ min _____ sec	_____ min _____ sec

List	Spelling Pattern	First Sort	Second Sort	Third Sort
		_____ min _____ sec	_____ min _____ sec	_____ min _____ sec
		_____ min _____ sec	_____ min _____ sec	_____ min _____ sec
		_____ min _____ sec	_____ min _____ sec	_____ min _____ sec
		_____ min _____ sec	_____ min _____ sec	_____ min _____ sec
		_____ min _____ sec	_____ min _____ sec	_____ min _____ sec
		_____ min _____ sec	_____ min _____ sec	_____ min _____ sec
		_____ min _____ sec	_____ min _____ sec	_____ min _____ sec
		_____ min _____ sec	_____ min _____ sec	_____ min _____ sec

List	Spelling Pattern	First Sort	Second Sort	Third Sort
		_____ min _____ sec	_____ min _____ sec	_____ min _____ sec
		_____ min _____ sec	_____ min _____ sec	_____ min _____ sec
		_____ min _____ sec	_____ min _____ sec	_____ min _____ sec
		_____ min _____ sec	_____ min _____ sec	_____ min _____ sec
		_____ min _____ sec	_____ min _____ sec	_____ min _____ sec
		_____ min _____ sec	_____ min _____ sec	_____ min _____ sec
		_____ min _____ sec	_____ min _____ sec	_____ min _____ sec
		_____ min _____ sec	_____ min _____ sec	_____ min _____ sec

Rate it!
Color in stars to show your rating.

	Title	Rate it!
1.		☆ ☆ ☆
2.		☆ ☆ ☆
3.		☆ ☆ ☆
4.		☆ ☆ ☆
5.		☆ ☆ ☆
6.		☆ ☆ ☆
7.		☆ ☆ ☆
8.		☆ ☆ ☆
9.		☆ ☆ ☆
10.		☆ ☆ ☆

Way to go! Color the 10 badge in your badge book.

MY READING LOG

	Title	Rate it! Color in stars to show your rating.		
11.		☆	☆	☆
12.		☆	☆	☆
13.		☆	☆	☆
14.		☆	☆	☆
15.		☆	☆	☆
16.		☆	☆	☆
17.		☆	☆	☆
18.		☆	☆	☆
19.		☆	☆	☆
20.		☆	☆	☆

Good job!   Color the **20** badge in your badge book.

Rate it!
Color in stars to show
your rating.

	Title			
21.		☆	☆	☆
22.		☆	☆	☆
23.		☆	☆	☆
24.		☆	☆	☆
25.		☆	☆	☆
26.		☆	☆	☆
27.		☆	☆	☆
28.		☆	☆	☆
29.		☆	☆	☆
30.		☆	☆	☆

Yes!   Color the (30) badge in your badge book.

Title	Rate it! Color in stars to show your rating.		
31.	☆	☆	☆
32.	☆	☆	☆
33.	☆	☆	☆
34.	☆	☆	☆
35.	☆	☆	☆
36.	☆	☆	☆
37.	☆	☆	☆
38.	☆	☆	☆
39.	☆	☆	☆
40.	☆	☆	☆

Hooray! Color the **40** badge in your badge book.

Rate it!
Color in stars to show
your rating.

	Title	
41.		☆ ☆ ☆
42.		☆ ☆ ☆
43.		☆ ☆ ☆
44.		☆ ☆ ☆
45.		☆ ☆ ☆
46.		☆ ☆ ☆
47.		☆ ☆ ☆
48.		☆ ☆ ☆
49.		☆ ☆ ☆
50.		☆ ☆ ☆

Fantastic!   Color the 50 badge in your badge book.

MY READING LOG

Title	Rate it! Color in stars to show your rating.
51.	☆ ☆ ☆
52.	☆ ☆ ☆
53.	☆ ☆ ☆
54.	☆ ☆ ☆
55.	☆ ☆ ☆
56.	☆ ☆ ☆
57.	☆ ☆ ☆
58.	☆ ☆ ☆
59.	☆ ☆ ☆
60.	☆ ☆ ☆

Cool! Color the 60 badge in your badge book.

	Title	Rate it! Color in stars to show your rating.
61.		☆ ☆ ☆
62.		☆ ☆ ☆
63.		☆ ☆ ☆
64.		☆ ☆ ☆
65.		☆ ☆ ☆
66.		☆ ☆ ☆
67.		☆ ☆ ☆
68.		☆ ☆ ☆
69.		☆ ☆ ☆
70.		☆ ☆ ☆

Awesome! Color the 70 badge in your badge book.

Rate it!
Color in stars to show your rating.

	Title	Rate it!
71.		☆ ☆ ☆
72.		☆ ☆ ☆
73.		☆ ☆ ☆
74.		☆ ☆ ☆
75.		☆ ☆ ☆
76.		☆ ☆ ☆
77.		☆ ☆ ☆
78.		☆ ☆ ☆
79.		☆ ☆ ☆
80.		☆ ☆ ☆

Wow!   Color the (80) badge in your badge book.

Rate it!
Color in stars to show
your rating.

	Title	
81.		☆ ☆ ☆
82.		☆ ☆ ☆
83.		☆ ☆ ☆
84.		☆ ☆ ☆
85.		☆ ☆ ☆
86.		☆ ☆ ☆
87.		☆ ☆ ☆
88.		☆ ☆ ☆
89.		☆ ☆ ☆
90.		☆ ☆ ☆

Amazing!   Color the 90 badge in your badge book.

MY READING LOG

	Title	Rate it! Color in stars to show your rating.
91.		☆ ☆ ☆
92.		☆ ☆ ☆
93.		☆ ☆ ☆
94.		☆ ☆ ☆
95.		☆ ☆ ☆
96.		☆ ☆ ☆
97.		☆ ☆ ☆
98.		☆ ☆ ☆
99.		☆ ☆ ☆
100.		☆ ☆ ☆

Superstar! Color the 100 badge in your badge book.

A-14

Back Cover

Fold on dotted line

Front Cover

Name

MY
BADGE
BOOK

Reading Log Badges

100

900

Fold on dotted line

Unit Badges

BEARS

INSECTS

PROBLEMS AND SOLUTIONS

DINOSAURS

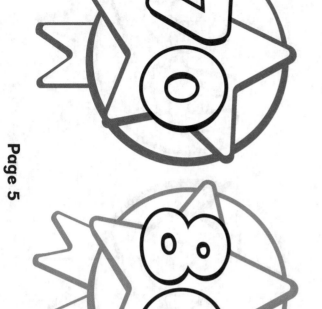

Fold on dotted line

CELEBRATE WHO WE ARE

INTERESTING PEOPLE

SADIQ AND THE DESERT STAR

FABLES

Reading Log Badges

20

10

40

30

Fold on dotted line

Unit Badges

AWESOME ANIMALS

STORIES OLD AND NEW

ANIMAL HELPERS

ANCIENT ROME

A-18